CONTENTS

TCHAIKOVSKY FAMILY

The Tchaikovsky family lived in Votkinsk, an iron mining town in Russia about 950 km east of Moscow. Ancestors of the family were nobility and may have come from Poland. Great-grandfather Tchaikovsky was an officer in the Cossacks during the reign of Peter the Great. Grandfather Tchaikovsky was a high-ranking member of the government. Peter's father, Ilya, was a government mining engineer.

ILYA TCHAIKOVSKY

In 1837, Ilya was offered a prestigious job as manager of the ironworks in Votkinsk. By then he was also an official in the government mining department in St Petersburg, Russia's capital city.

▶ *Ilya Tchaikovsky was also a magistrate and held the honorary title of Major General. He had an army of 100 Cossack soldiers under his command.*

FAMOUS CHILDHOODS

Peter Ilyich
TCHAIKOVSKY

Barrie Carson Turner

Chrysalis Children's Books

First published in the UK in 2003 by

Chrysalis Children's Books
64 Brewery Road, London N7 9NT

Copyright © Chrysalis Books PLC 2003
Text by Barrie Carson Turner

ISBN 184138 6960

British Library Cataloguing in Publication Data for this
book is available from the British Library.

A BELITHA BOOK

Editorial Manager: Joyce Bentley
Senior Editor: Sarah Nunn
Editorial Assistant: Clare Chambers
Picture researcher: Jenny Barlow

Produced by
Tall Tree Ltd
Editor: Jon Richards
Designer: Dean Price
Consultant: Yvonne Dix

Printed in China

10 9 8 7 6 5 4 3 2 1

PICTURE CREDITS

All reasonable efforts have been made to trace the relevant
copyright holders of the images contained within this book.
If we were unable to reach you, please contact Chrysalis Books.

B = bottom; *C* = centre; *L* = left; *R* = right; *T* = top.
Cover *background* AKG London *front* Mary Evans Picture Library *back* AKG
London **1** AKG London **2** AKG London **4** Novosti (London) **5** *T* AKG
London *B* The Art Archive/Musée de L'Armée, Paris/Dagli Orti **6** Mary Evans
Picture Library **7** *T* Novosti (London) *B* Corbis/Wolfgang Kaehler **8** Novosti
(London) **9** *T* Novosti (London) *B* The Art Archive/Musée de la Révolution
Française, Vizille/Dagli Orti **10** AKG London **11** *T* Mary Evans Picture Library
B The Art Archive/Museo Bibliografico Musicale, Bologna/Dagli Orti (A)
12 The Art Archive/Society of the Friends of Music, Vienna/Dagli Orti (A)
13 *T* The Art Archive/Musée du Louvre, Paris/Dagli Orti (A) *B* AKG
London/Vsevolod M. Arsenyev **14** AKG London/Tretjakov Gallery, Moscow
15 *T* Hulton Archive *B* The Art Archive/Bibliothèque Municipale, Dijon/Dagli
Orti **16** AKG London/State Russian Museum, St. Petersburg **17** *T* and *B* Mary
Evans Picture Library **18** AKG London **19** *T* (see 2) *B* AKG London **20** AKG
London/Pushkin Museum, Moscow **21** *T* Novosti (London) *B* The Art
Archive/Tretjakov Gallery, Moscow/Dagli Orti (A) **22** The Art Archive/Galleria
d'Arte Moderna, Piacenza/Dagli Orti (A) **23** *T* (see cover *background*) *B* (see 1)
24 Novosti (London) **25** *T* (see cover *back*) *B* Novosti (London)
26 Corbis/Reproduced by permission of The State Hermitage Museum,
St. Petersburg, Russia **27** *T* and *B* Novosti (London) **28** (see cover *front*)
28-29 *background* AKG London **29** Novosti (London) **30** (see 1)
30-31 *background* (see 28-29 *background*) **31** (see 14).

ALEXANDRA TCHAIKOVSKY

Peter's mother, Alexandra Andreyevna Tchaikovsky, was cultured, musical and well educated, and could speak French and German fluently. Her grandparents were French, but had left France after the outbreak of the French revolution in 1789. She gave Peter a love of French music and all things French.

▶ *Alexandra Andreyevna married Ilya in 1833 and was his second wife.*

COSSACKS

The Cossack people came from southern Russia. They were horsemen in the Russian army. They wore unusual, brimless hats that widened at the top.

◀ *Cossack soldiers were known for their determination and bravery.*

A GENIUS IN THE MAKING

Pater gave many of his compositions attractive French titles, such as Sérénade Mélancolique (Sad Serenade) for violin and orchestra, and his piano pieces Les Saisons (The Seasons).

PETER IS BORN

Peter Ilyich Tchaikovsky was born on 7 May 1840. The Tchaikovsky household was large, and there were many servants. Peter was the second child in the family. His elder brother, Nikolay, was born in 1838. In 1843, a sister, Alexandra, was born, and in 1844 another boy, Ippolit, arrived. Finally, twin boys, Anatoly and Modest, were born in 1850. The rest of the household was made up of a stepsister, Zinaida, from Ilya's previous marriage, two cousins and an elderly aunt.

▲ *The home in Votkinsk where Peter was born.*

PETER'S BIRTHPLACE

The Tchaikovskys were well respected in Votkinsk, and since Ilya's job was well paid, money was never a problem. The large, imposing family house reflected the respectable social standing of Ilya.

A GENIUS IN THE MAKING

Peter's first musical experience was hearing his mother sing while accompanying herself on the piano. Influenced by this, Peter wrote almost a hundred songs.

MINING

During the mid-nineteenth century, Russia was desperately trying to industrialize. A major part of this process was the mining of raw materials. Peter's father oversaw this work in the mines around Votkinsk.

◀ *An iron-ore mine in nineteenth-century Russia.*

THE URAL MOUNTAINS

Votkinsk is situated in the beautiful and mineral-rich Ural Mountains that run north to south through western Russia. The mountains stretch for 2500 km and divide Europe from Asia.

▶ *Much of the Ural Mountain range is covered in thick forest.*

A New Governess

Peter showed an interest in music from an early age. One time, when his mother was visiting her family in St Petersburg, Ilya wrote to her, saying Peter and his sister Alexandra (who was only 19 months old at the time) had composed a song called *Our Mama in Petersburg*. Peter couldn't read or play a note of music, yet he was already composing!

YOUNGER SISTER

Peter's sister Alexandra was known as Sacha by the family. She was almost three years younger than Peter. From an early age, and throughout their lives, the two were very close.

▶ *Peter's sister, Alexandra Tchaikovsky, in later life, with her husband, Lev Davidov.*

A GENIUS IN THE MAKING

Peter's new governess introduced him to literature and poetry, which he grew to love. Three of his overtures, Romeo and Juliet, The Tempest *and* Hamlet, *were inspired by Shakespeare plays.*

FANNY DURBACH

Peter's parents hired a governess, a young Frenchwoman called Fanny Durbach, to teach his older brother Nikolay and his cousin Lydia. But Peter insisted on joining in the lessons, too. The children's new governess taught her pupils French and German, as well as general subjects.

▶ *Fanny Durbach, who became Peter's governess in 1844.*

THE FRENCH REVOLUTION

Fanny's history lessons no doubt included stories of the terrors of the French revolution, which caused so many French people, including Peter's great-grandparents, to flee to the safety of other countries in Europe.

◀ *This painting shows the storming of the Bastille during the French revolution.*

MECHANICAL MARVEL

Votkinsk was not a musical town, but the Tchaikovsky family owned a piano and Peter frequently heard his mother playing and singing. Ilya was no musician, but he enjoyed listening to music. However, Peter's interest in music was stirred by the arrival of a new mechanical marvel into the Tchaikovsky household.

THE ORCHESTRION

One day, following a visit by Ilya to St Petersburg, a large box arrived at the Tchaikovsky house. It contained an orchestrion – a machine that looked and worked like a large musical box.

▶ *The orchestrion changed Peter's life. As an adult looking back, he said the orchestrion gave him his first real musical experience.*

—— *A GENIUS IN THE MAKING* ——

The music of Mozart was very special to Peter. In 1887 he wrote a piece based on several melodies by Mozart, which he called Mozartiana.

ZERLINA

Peter fell in love with the orchestrion. It played a selection of operatic melodies, including music by the composers Bellini, Rossini, Donizetti and Mozart. Peter's favourite melody was an aria sung by Zerlina, from Mozart's opera *Don Giovanni*.

◀ *The character of Zerlina is a peasant girl who the main character, Don Giovanni, tries to seduce on her wedding day.*

WOLFGANG AMADEUS MOZART

The Austrian composer Wolfgang Amadeus Mozart was particularly famous for his operas. The orchestrion played several pieces from his opera *Don Giovanni*. Mozart wrote a huge range of music including operas, symphonies, concertos, chamber music and piano pieces. Peter later wrote 'it was due to Mozart that I devoted my life to music.'

▶ *Wolfgang Amadeus Mozart lived from 1756 to 1791.*

PIANO LESSONS

Peter, now six, was no longer happy just to listen to his favourite tunes on the orchestrion. He wanted to play them himself, so he began picking out the tunes on the family piano. He also started making up his own pieces, although he didn't know how to write these down yet. Seeing his interest in the piano, his parents decided that it was time to begin Peter's piano lessons, and so they found a local teacher, Mariya Palchikova, to teach him.

◄ *Fryderyk Chopin (1810-1849) is best known for his piano pieces, which include many waltzes, polonaises and mazurkas.*

FRYDERYK CHOPIN

Soon Peter was playing simple pieces by Fryderyk Chopin, who, at the time, was considered to be a very modern composer. Chopin was also a concert pianist and the majority of his pieces were for the piano. His music is full of the rhythms and melodies of his native Poland.

A GENIUS IN THE MAKING

In 1878-1879 Peter wrote an opera based on the story of Joan of Arc, that he called The Maid of Orleans. *It was not a success, although it was the first of Peter's operas to be performed abroad.*

JOAN OF ARC

By the age of six, Peter had a good grasp of French and German. He also studied literature and wrote some French poetry, including a poem about Joan of Arc.

◄ *Joan of Arc (1412-1431) became a French heroine during the Hundred Years War against England.*

▲ *The family piano in the Tchaikovsky museum in Votkinsk.*

THE FAMILY PIANO

Peter greatly enjoyed his piano lessons and learnt quickly. Within three years he could sight-read – that is to play music never seen before – better than his teacher. The Tchaikovsky family piano has been preserved in the house in Votkinsk, which is now a museum.

THE MOVE TO MOSCOW

In 1848, Ilya heard of an exciting new job in Moscow. It offered greater financial rewards than his present job, and the position would almost certainly be his for the asking. Ilya felt that the slight risk of things not turning out was worth taking and so he resigned from his post in Votkinsk. He packed up the house and started the family on the journey to a new life.

ARRIVAL IN MOSCOW

Terrible news awaited the family's arrival in Moscow. The position that Ilya had been so convinced was his had already been filled. Worse still, it had been taken by a friend with whom he had shared details of the appointment. Ilya was now jobless!

◀ *The journey to Moscow took 12 tiring days.*

THE BOLSHOI THEATRE

The move from Votkinsk was very upsetting for the family. Peter, especially, was devastated at having to leave his governess who had almost become a member of the family. But Moscow would not be without its pleasures and excitements. There was great music to be heard at the spectacular Bolshoi Theatre.

▶ *The Bolshoi Theatre in Moscow hosted concerts, ballets and operas.*

CHOLERA EPIDEMIC

In the end, Moscow did not become a home for the family. In fact, the move had risked the health of all. The city was in the grip of a terrible and deadly cholera epidemic, and it was dangerous to stay. Fearing infection, Ilya took his family to St Petersburg.

◀ *The cholera outbreak not only brought danger from infection, but also from violence from people desperate for food and medicine.*

A GENIUS IN THE MAKING

Peter loved the sound of an orchestra. In the Dance of the Sugar-Plum Fairy, *he introduced a new instrument, the celesta, which makes a high ringing sound like miniature bells.*

MOVING ON TO THE CAPITAL

I n St Petersburg, Peter was enrolled in a fashionable new boarding school, the Schmelling school. But he was badly bullied and hated being there. He began piano lessons with a new piano teacher, but within a few weeks he and his brother caught the measles and had to stay at home for six months.

THE RUSSIAN CAPITAL

St Petersburg was the capital of Russia, and Peter was astonished to see the grandness of the buildings there. Fortunately, his mother Alexandra had a sister in the city, so the family did not feel so far away from home.

▲ *The Russian capital of St Petersburg at the time when Peter and his family moved there.*

RUSSIAN PEASANTS

Travelling from Votkinsk to Moscow and then on to St Petersburg gave Peter his first real glimpse of the Russian countryside. The majority of people in Russia at the time were peasants who did not own any land or possessions.

▶ *A boy from a well-to-do family like Peter's would have barely been aware of the poverty of most of the Russian population.*

FAMILY PHOTOGRAPH

Friends must have been astonished to see this picture of the Tchaikovsky family, taken when photography was in its infancy. Peter, aged eight, is standing next to his mother. The twins had not been born when the photograph was taken.

◀ *This photograph of the family was taken in 1848. Peter stands on the far left.*

A GENIUS IN THE MAKING

Peter was very interested in the folk music of his country, music that played an important part in the life of Russian peasants. Peter's second symphony is known as the Little Russian *because of the Russian melodies in it.*

LAW SCHOOL

Ilya finally found work in the town of Alapayevsk and the family moved there, but the time soon came for Peter to chose a career. Boys from high-ranking families in Russia usually went into the army or civil service. Ilya did not think that music was an acceptable career for his son, so it was decided that Peter should study law. In the summer of 1850, Peter left Alapayevsk and travelled with his mother back to St Petersburg to be enrolled in the School of Jurisprudence.

RUSSIAN MILITARY

It was clear to Ilya that Peter was artistic. The army, with its harsh uncultured lifestyle, would almost certainly have been a bad choice of profession for Peter. Perhaps Ilya deliberately chose a gentler career for his son.

▶ *Russian cavalry of the nineteenth century.*

A GENIUS IN THE MAKING

A great part of Peter's musical gift was a flair for the unusual. The second movement of his Pathétique symphony has five beats to the bar, instead of the usual three or four. This was extremely unusual in its day.

TSAR NICHOLAS I

Working in the Tsar's legal department, which is the role that Peter was now training for, would require tact and delicacy. In Russia, the law was the Tsar and there was no parliament. The Tsar had a series of advisers, and with them he made the laws. But the Tsar always had the final say.

◀ *Tsar Nicholas I was the ruler of Russia from 1825 to 1855.*

▲ *The Winter Palace in St Petersburg was the seat of the royal court and home of the Tsar.*

CHOOSING A SCHOOL

Ilya was thinking ahead when he chose a school for his son. In less than ten years Peter would be starting work, so what better place to send him than Russia's capital city, St Petersburg.

A Visit to the Opera

Having arrived in St Petersburg, Peter's mother stayed several weeks with him before returning home. She took him to see *A Life for the Tsar*, an opera by the Russian composer Mikhail Ivanovich Glinka.

A Russian opera

Glinka (1804-1857) wrote *A Life for the Tsar* to demonstrate that opera could have a Russian story and Russian music. Italian opera was very popular in Russia at the time – there was no Russian opera. Glinka felt that Russians deserved their own music too, and set about writing it.

◄ *Before becoming a composer, Glinka had worked as a government official, just as Peter would do in a few years' time.*

A VERY RUSSIAN STORY

A Life for the Tsar made a powerful impression on Peter. The opera tells of a Polish plot to kill the Tsar. A peasant, Ivan Susanin, tricks the invading armies and saves the Tsar, but loses his own life.

▶ *The opera is set during the Russian-Polish wars of the seventeenth century.*

MUSIC MAKING

In St Petersburg, Peter and his mother stayed with relatives who were good amateur musicians. It was a time of musical parties with family and friends.

◀ *A musical party in a nineteenth-century Russian house.*

A GENIUS IN THE MAKING

Like Glinka, Peter was determined to compose his own Russian operas, and he did. The opera Vakula the Blacksmith *is a fairy tale set in Russia at Christmas.*

A Death in the Family

In 1852, Ilya retired and the family joined Peter in St Petersburg. Everyone was together again or at least close, since Peter remained at boarding school. But then, tragedy struck the family.

▲ *A nineteenth-century Russian funeral.*

THE DEATH OF PETER'S MOTHER

In June 1854, Peter's mother died of cholera. Peter was closer to his mother than anyone else in the family. For comfort, he turned to music. He had often improvised pieces at the piano, but now he wrote his very first compositions down.

A GENIUS IN THE MAKING

After the death of his mother, Peter wrote his first known composition, which was a waltz. Waltz tunes, such as the famous Dance of the Flowers, *appear in many of his works.*

FUNERAL MUSIC

His mother's death was to haunt Peter for many years. The *Pathétique* symphony, the last symphony Peter wrote, has music from the Russian funeral service in it, probably as a memorial to his mother.

◀ *Peter wrote his* Pathétique *symphony in 1893, some 39 years after his mother's death.*

DESPAIR

Looking back as an adult on the death of his mother, Peter said that he was only saved from insanity by his love of music. Throughout his life he turned to music in times of sadness.

▶ *This photograph of Peter was taken in 1890.*

MUSIC AND POETRY

During his early years in law school, Peter gradually lost interest in the piano. His piano teachers changed frequently and, one by one, they tired of trying to teach a boy who didn't want to learn. But after his mother's death, things changed. Peter was again interested in music, especially composition.

AN ITALIAN SONG

When he was 16, Peter began singing lessons. His teacher was the Italian Luigi Piccioli, who also encouraged Peter to compose. In 1865, Peter wrote an Italian song called *Mezze Notte* that became his first published composition.

▶ *Luigi Piccioli was a retired opera singer who hated all types of music except for Italian opera.*

DANCE MUSIC

Peter's formal piano lessons were not progressing very satisfactorily. But he enjoyed playing popular music and could improvise well. This made him the perfect party guest to provide the music for dances and other social events.

▶ *Russian dances were usually lively events.*

A GENIUS IN THE MAKING

One of Peter's piano teachers, Rudolf Kündinger, told Ilya that his son had little musical ability. Little did he know that Peter would later become one of the world's most famous composers.

LIFELONG FRIEND

During his years in the school of law Peter made several good friends, including Alexander Apukhtin, who became a poet and supplied the words for many of Peter's songs.

◀ *Alexander Apukhtin and Peter are next to each other in the middle of this photograph.*

SCHOOL ENDS

On 13 May 1859, Peter graduated from school. He was 13th in his class and had done well. He began working for the Ministry of Justice, but he found his job as a clerk extremely boring, although it was nice to be earning money for the first time.

◄ *The Grand Duchess Elena Pavlovna was an aunt of the Tsar.*

RUSSIAN MUSIC SOCIETY

A few months after Peter left school a new musical establishment, the Russian Music Society, was set up in St Petersburg. Its creator was the influential and wealthy Grand Duchess Elena Pavlovna. The goal of the society was to encourage the study of music and performance in Russia.

A GENIUS IN THE MAKING

While studying at the Conservatoire, Peter wrote an overture called The Storm, *which was his first large piece for orchestra. This music is now forgotten, but another overture,* 1812, *has become one of his most famous pieces.*

▲ *Today, the Mikhailovsky Palace is a museum.*

MIKHAILOVSKY PALACE

At first, the Russian Music Society had nowhere from which to operate. So the Grand Duchess generously offered rooms in her own home, the Mikhailovsky Palace. Peter enrolled for composition lessons with the composer Nikolay Zaremba.

ST PETERSBURG CONSERVATOIRE OF MUSIC

The Tsar, who had previously given financial support to the Music Society, was delighted when the venture was a success. In 1862, he offered more funds that allowed the society to move into its own premises. It now changed its name to the St Petersburg Conservatoire of Music.

◄ *The St Petersburg Conservatoire of Music.*

PETER'S LEGACY

In 1863, Peter finally decided to leave the law and make a career in music, so he enrolled into the Conservatoire as a full-time student. His new composition teacher was the pianist and composer, Anton Rubinstein. Peter's brother Nikolay was appalled at the change in career. Peter wrote to him, 'I may not be another Glinka, but I promise you that you will some day be proud to have me as your brother.'

THE FULL-TIME COMPOSER

The St Petersburg Conservatoire allowed Russian music students to be educated in their own country for the first time. It was no longer necessary to travel to other parts of Europe to study. Peter was the first Russian composer to be educated in Russia, and the first Russian to be a full-time composer.

▶ *In his final years, Peter achieved international fame in Europe and North America as both a conductor and composer.*

▲ *Peter's signature*

A GENEROUS FRIEND

In 1876, Peter received a letter from an unknown woman. She was Nadia von Meck, a wealthy widow. She liked Peter's music and for 14 years supported him financially, even though the two of them never met. But despite this financial security, Peter's life was seldom happy. He died in St Petersburg on 6 November 1893, possibly from suicide. Today, Peter Ilyich Tchaikovsky is probably remembered most of all for his beautiful melodies and strong romantic harmonies.

◀ *Peter's statue in Moscow.*

A GENIUS IN THE MAKING

Peter Ilyich Tchaikovsky wrote operas, symphonies, concertos, ballets, orchestral pieces, chamber music, piano pieces and songs.

GLOSSARY

ARIA
A song that is often part of a larger work, such as an opera.

BALLET MUSIC
Music written for dancers to perform to on the stage.

CELESTA
An instrument that looks and is played like a small piano, but which makes a high ringing sound like miniature bells.

CONCERT
When players or singers perform in front of an audience.

CONCERTO
A piece usually written for one instrument that is accompanied by an orchestra.

FOLK MUSIC
The traditional songs and dance music of a country. The music is usually so old that its composers are not known.

IMPROVISE
To make up the music as you play it.

MAZURKA
A rhythmic and lively Polish dance with three beats to the bar.

MUSICIAN
Someone who plays an instrument or sings.

OPERA

A musical play in which actors sing their parts. The singers are usually accompanied by an orchestra.

OVERTURE

A piece of music that introduces a major work, such as an opera, or a piece of music that has been inspired by a particular scene or story.

PERFORM

To play or sing music or act out a play in front of an audience.

POLONAISE

A lively Polish dance with three beats to the bar.

SERENADE

Traditionally a love song, usually with gentle and quiet music.

SIGHT-READ

Play music 'on sight', never having seen it before.

SYMPHONY

A composition for orchestra, usually made up of four movements.

WALTZ

A ballroom dance that has three beats to the bar.

INDEX